# BEFORE
# SHE
# IS
# GONE

by

Russell Clack

*Before She is Gone*

Copyright © 2016 A. Russell Clack

ISBN-13: 978-1533212092

ISBN-10: 1533212090

First Edition 2016 CreateSpace

# ACKNOWLEDGMENTS

I AM DEEPLY INDEBTED to Mark McKenzie and Melissa Coleman McNulty who painstakingly reviewed, corrected, and made invaluable suggestions to make this more readable and to Stacy Tyson of Truth Seekers Fellowship for his efforts in getting this story formatted for publication.

I wish to thank my longtime mentor, confidant and friend, Dr. Michael Kerns of Barnabas and Associates, who has been an encouragement to me in more ways than he will ever know. His writing the book *Worth Works* inspired me to put these thoughts on paper.

Men in three prayer groups have prayed for and built me up when I have been discouraged: The First Evangelical Church Monday Prayer Breakfast, the Thursday morning prayer group and the Friday Morning men's group have all been essential in keeping me focused. The Friday group has graciously allowed me to go through the material presented here, taking one section at a time. Thanks to these men for their interest and their comments, particularly Thomas Mayberry,

Gene Lambert, Jim Pendleton, Doug Barron and Carlyle Acosta of the Friday group.

Further encouragement has also come from the pastor of the Refuge Church, Scott Benjamin, as well as brothers in Christ Clayton Poff, Doug Schoenfield, John Adams, Jerry Salley, Chad Mitchell, and Martin Jones.

Most of all, thanks go to God who took a foolish, prideful man and lifted him up out of the pit of destruction, out of the miry clay and set his feet upon the rock—Jesus the Christ. He truly restored the years the locust had eaten. Praise God for His Mercy and Grace. May He be glorified by what is written here.

# MY PRAYER

**FATHER**, I pray that the words written here will be used to bring husbands and wives close to you. I pray that they will be Your words and not mine, that the Holy Spirit will speak to each one who reads them and will meet whatever need they have so that their marriages will glorify You. Heal marriages Lord, unify couples, have them love You more and love each other more. Thank You for what You have done and for what You are going to do.

# FORWARD

**As I was sitting home alone** a few months after my wife Barbara passed away, I was reflecting on our lives together. In the 53 years we were married, we went through four different stages in our marriage relationship. I call them the "Beginning" years, the "Doubting" years, the "Dark" years and the "Great" years.

Those words are so ordinary sounding and do not adequately portray our lives together, but they serve a useful purpose. Useful because they describe four major periods in our marriage. Useful because you may use them to question which stage you and your wife are in. Hopefully you are in the "great" years of your marriage, but I know that is not the case with most marriages that I have observed. Most seem to be stuck just living, taking their lives together for granted, and not thinking anything tragic will happen to them.

Husbands, I encourage you to question where you are in your marriage. Be proactive, take action. Work hard on your marriage. It will be well worth it.

We married seven months after we met on a blind date and didn't really know each other that well (even though we thought we did). The first few years ("Beginning" years) were spent getting to know and understand each other better, adjusting our lives to our different ways and peculiarities, and having two children born into the family. In addition, we went from her working to support us during my last year in college at Chapel Hill, to my first full-time job in Wilmington NC where our first boy was born, to the Washington DC area where our second boy was born. Then I changed occupations within the Public Health service and we were transferred to Memphis, Tn. The changes, the arrival of two active babies 18 months apart and the moves caused me to start "Doubting" that my marriage to Barbara was what God had wanted. I wasn't sure it was what I wanted.

The distractions, the new job in Memphis, Barbara's focus on the children and not on me all contributed to my dissatisfaction with the marriage. I felt we were going separate ways and were drifting apart. The doubts continued and became stronger. Even though I lived in the same house with her I began to think that the only thing we had in common was our two boys, who we both loved very much. This thinking resulted in me "straying" from home (the "Dark" years) and finding a girlfriend. The affair lasted for 10 years.

I became a Christian during these "Dark" years and eventually felt led to obey the scriptures. I stopped seeing my girlfriend and began making a real commitment to my wife Barbara. These remaining years of our lives together (the "Great" years) were so filled with love, so fulfilling that I have felt led to share our journey with family, friends and other husbands in the hope that I can prevent others from traveling the same dark path I traveled.

As I was thinking about Barbara, it occurred to me as to how much different our family's lives would have been if we had divorced, or if she had died during those first three stages of our married life. What regrets, what sorrows I would have had. How different all of us would have been. I am so grateful we made it to the fourth stage, the "Great" years, of our lives. It was only through God's grace and the forgiving love of my wife that we had a great, great marriage.

What about your marriage? How would you feel if it ended tomorrow? What if your wife died in a car wreck today? Would you have deep regrets? Great sorrow? Would there have been something you should have told her? Did you leave her this morning after an argument? Have you started having doubts about being married to your wife? Have you been spending time with someone other than your wife because she neglects you to take care of the children? Are you in "Dark" years?

We do not know when we will pass from this life to the next. But we do know that death is a certainty. We don't need the Bible to tell us that it is appointed unto man once to die and after that comes the judgment. We see it all around us. The first thing we need to make certain is where we will spend eternity. We will talk more about this later.

The second thing we husbands need to do is focus on how we treat our wives. This is the person God gave us as our helper, our companion, and the one we expect to grow old with. Unfortunately life sometimes throws us curves and we find we have taken different paths from the ones we intended to take. Paths that bring discouragement, anger, fear and heartbreak into our lives and into the lives of those we love. I hope and pray that what I am writing here will make you think. Will make you question. Will make you examine your relationship with your wife right now, at this point in time. Where is it? Is it where you want it to be?

I want to share the things I have learned from being able to spend the better part of my life loving and being loved by my wife. I do this in the hope that you will put into practice what I have learned and that you will have the greatest marriage possible. Not just for you, but for your extended family as well as others. A great marriage is encouraging to many people. It gives people hope and it gives others the desire to have the same relationship you have. Great marriages change people. Examine your marriage. Examine what you can do to make it great.

Before it's too late.

*Before she is gone.*

# INTRODUCTION

**MY 77 YEAR OLD WIFE BARBARA** died January 29, 2015 of dementia, which she had for about six years. Her life was one of devotion and love for her husband, her children, grandchildren, her friends and love for God and His Son Jesus.

When we men first start out on our life's adventure of marriage, we seldom think about our wife being incapacitated or dying prematurely. Like almost all couples Barbara and I know, life was full of promise, expectations were high and we were eager to make an impact on each other and on our world. After the first thrill of marriage, we got caught up in work, in raising children and in purchasing the necessities and the not so necessities of life. We got caught up in just being busy, filling our time with all sorts of activities. Like most humans, even when the thought of death occurs to us it is quickly dismissed. We don't want to think about it or face it. Unless we are already in a life threatening situation, it's easy to think about it as being sometime far off into the future. Even if we are church-goers, when the pastor starts talking about death we almost instinctively start thinking about something else and not paying attention to what he is saying. Needless to say, the thought of the death of our wife is not something we husbands want to face.

Hopefully what is being written on these pages will cause you to stop and think of the subject of your wife's death. I know that even as I write this, your mind is rejecting the thought. Don't let it. Hear and understand what is being said. It is too important.

I was very blessed to be married to my wife for 53 years. In today's world that is uncommon. Divorce, death, disease, stresses of life and going in different ways cause most marriages to end earlier than ours. I thank the Lord for keeping us together even when, humanly speaking, we should have divorced because of my uncaring, selfish and adulterous life style. Yes, she should have left me, but she stayed with me and loved me back into loving her through her patience and grace. All because God gave her those qualities. When God and Barbara finally got my attention, we had a great life together for many, many years.

I want to share with you some of what God and Barbara taught me as a result of our staying together.

Husbands, you need to realize that the lives of you and your wife are like a vapor, subject to being over at any moment. You will not get a phone call, a text message or an email that death is about to occur. Hopefully you two will live a long, prosperous and fruitful life together but there is no guarantee that will happen.

Once your wife passes, you will get no more chances to say or do things for her and with her that you always intended to do but were too busy. Keep these thoughts and words in mind as you read through the following pages. One note: this is not meant to be a chronological narrative of events. Rather, it is a series of topics to be read individually, examining where you stand on each point and then resolving to change your attitudes and your actions. Do what you need to do to make your marriage great.

Husbands, you are to love your wife, forgive her, protect her, serve her, give to her, encourage her, be her friend, pray for her, make God central in your lives, commit to her, respect her, communicate with her and make love to her. Each one of these will be discussed in the following pages.

It's a tall order but if you are not doing these things, you need to start.

Now.

Today.

# HUSBAND, LOVE YOUR WIFE

"**HUSBANDS, LOVE YOUR WIVES.**" I had read these words in the Bible, Colossians Chapter 3 many times but they had never made an impact on me. At least not until I was about eight years into an adulterous affair. The first few years Barbara and I were married were good years but she soon began to invest most of her time and energy into our two rambunctious boys. They were a handful, being only eighteen months apart. At that time I was a spoiled mama's boy, only child, naturally self-centered and resented her lack of attention to me. I convinced myself that the only reason she married me was to "marry a college boy" who would provide for her and that she really didn't love me. I began to think our marriage wasn't ordained by God and I began believing He had another mate picked out for me. Husbands, it's easy to deceive yourselves. That way you can justify your actions.

Do NOT listen to those voices. Do NOT build up resentments against your wife. Do NOT keep that mental notebook you have been keeping. You know the one. The one where you have listed all those ways she has offended you, neglected you, nagged you, been mad at you. Those times she refused to have sex with you. All those times she didn't want to do something with you that you really wanted to do. You know what I'm writing about. Rip those thoughts from your mind. Forget them.

After a few years of her neglecting me (in my mind) I decided to find someone who would meet my needs. Someone who would love me for me. After all, I reasoned, God didn't want me with her, I did. I met Barbara on a blind date before I was a Christian and she danced like me, drank like me and partied like me. That's why I was attracted to her. That's why I married her. I thought God didn't have anything to do with it. I convinced myself I was right, I was justified in looking for someone else. After all, I was a good guy, doing more good things than bad. Oh, the deception, lies and wickedness in me.

So, I looked around and sure enough found someone.

We were going to church as all this was going on and my wife asked the pastor to come to our home to talk with me about Jesus. (Barbara didn't know about the affair at this point in time as it was early in the affair). She waited to tell me he was coming until he parked in front of the house and was walking up the driveway. I was sitting in my favorite chair drinking a beer and just had time to slide it under the chair before he came in. All my life I believed there was a God but had never believed that Jesus was God's Son, never believed that He lived a perfect sinless life on this earth, was crucified and buried for my sins and was raised up on the third day. I just didn't believe it. Maybe you don't either. Anyway, that night the pastor opened his Bible and shared a few verses with me and my nephew who was staying with us temporarily. All of a sudden, I knew. I KNEW that Jesus was God. All of a sudden I knew I was a sinful creature and that no matter how many good things I had done, I could not save myself by my good works. God opened my eyes and my heart. He revealed the TRUTH to me. I became a believer that night.

Just to show you how irrational my thinking was, the next day I had to talk to my girlfriend. I had to tell her what had happened to me and I HAD to ask her if she had accepted Jesus as her Savior. I was scared to ask, believing that if she said "no" I would have to stop seeing her. If she said "yes", then she was the one I was supposed to be married to. Awful thinking! Stupid thinking! Twisted, delusional thinking! But there I was.

My girlfriend said "yes" that she was a believer but had been away from church and from God. The next Sunday she started going to church and continued to go almost every Sunday. So, I took that as the sign that we were supposed to be together. In many ways we were soul mates, knowing what the other was thinking, showing up at the same places not knowing the other was going to be there, liking the same things, almost never arguing, talking together all the time. My perfect mate.

Only problem was, I was already married with two children.

My girlfriend and I grew closer together and also began growing closer to the Lord. I was still living at home with Barbara and our two boys and often tried to leave. I even moved out for about a month and stayed with a co-worker (male) but the guilt over leaving my boys was just too much. So I moved back home. All this time (or most of it) Barbara was still loving to me and always faithful. I don't see how she put up with me. I'm ashamed to admit it but my girlfriend would call the house at night and demand to speak to me, to tell me to either talk to her or go see her, right then. I would get up out of bed and go talk to her. Thinking about this and writing it down still causes me much pain as I think about how horrible I was to Barbara. Yet she stayed with me.

I continued to go to church and to bible study. I began maturing in the Word and in applying it to my life. Over time both my girlfriend and I became convinced that what we were doing was wrong and against God's will. We tried several times to stop seeing each other. It was hard because we were so alike, so close.

By this time my oldest boy was driving. One day after Thanksgiving the two boys were in a bad wreck because of an icy, slick road. My younger son was knocked unconscious and the older son had back injuries. Fortunately the back injuries turned out not to be serious, but we were told that the younger boy may never come out of his coma. Barbara and I began praying together before we would go into ICU to see him. After twelve days in ICU he was placed in a private room. The doctors hoped the room change would make a difference. If not, we were told that he would be permanently placed in a nursing facility and probably die there. But, as an answer to prayer, on the thirteenth day he woke up. Although he had difficulty walking and talking for about a month or so, he regained all of his functions.

Time went on and my girlfriend and I decided again to break up. Soon after that I was reading Colossians in my Bible and came across the verse that said "Husbands, love your wives." This time it really spoke to me. The words jumped out at me. I couldn't get them out of my mind. It was all I could see and think about. I realized this was a commandment from God Himself and if God gives us a commandment He also gives us a way to carry it out. I said "But God, I don't love my wife. You will have to show me how to do this." As I thought about it, I realized that the answer was very simple. I needed to treat her just like I had treated my girlfriend.

Guys, do you really, really love your wife? Have you gotten so settled into your marriage that it's just old stuff? Or are you like I was—questioning whether or not I was supposed to be married to her? Feeling trapped and wanting something or someone else. The Bible says "husbands, love your wives." Set your mind every day to do that. In some way show her that you love her EVERY DAY, even if you don't feel the love. Don't worry. God will provide it. Don't be led by your feelings.

God showed me that love is not just an emotion. It is not a "feeling." It is not lust. That is what the world and the flesh teach. Love is a commitment. It is an action, an act of the will. 1 Corinthians describes love best when it says (among other things) "love is patient, love is kind, love is not jealous, love is not selfish, love does not keep score of wrongs." I started trying to BE those things by DOING those things.

Here's what I did. Since Barbara didn't trust me, I started calling her every afternoon to tell her what time I was going to be home. If it was to be later than normal I would explain to her why I was going to be late. I would also call her again during that time if I was to be later than what I had told her. I made myself accountable to her. I stopped going out by myself on the weekends. I began to take her and the boys with me if I had to go somewhere. I took her on dates. We began dancing again and helped form the Memphis Shag Club. When I got home at night I asked her what went on that day and I LISTENED as she told me. I quit arguing with her and raising my voice at her. I started treating her as my equal instead of belittling her. I helped around the house (some). I talked with her and listened to her and got her opinion. We began making joint decisions.

I set my mind to love her. I treated her like I loved her. Soon the love came. Well, not so soon. About a year or more later I realized that I was really in love with the woman I had married and that beyond any doubt, she was the one God had picked for me. None of this means we didn't have our differences, because we did. That doesn't mean we didn't have arguments, because we did. We were not alike in many ways and it continued to cause us some difficulties. But I came to realize that was God's way of sandpapering us, making us more like Jesus. It also kept us from making too many unsound decisions. The differences between us were a blessing, not a curse.

As a result of all of this, I believe the last thirty five years of our marriage were the greatest they could have been. They were better than I had imagined they could be. God blessed our marriage. He blessed it with longevity so we could experience the joy of love as it is supposed to be. The Lord truly restored the years the locusts had eaten.

I can't help but think of what would have happened to me, to Barbara and to our boys and family if her life had ended during our difficult, "dark" years. What remorse and regrets I would have had. How guilty I would be. How different my children and grand-children's lives would have been if she had died early on.

I have no lasting regrets about our married life after God changed me and I am so thankful for that. I do have plenty though for putting her through what I put her through earlier. It makes me sick to think about the way I treated her. I know she forgave me. I have forgiven myself but the consequences of my actions are still being carried out.

The question is: How about you? Suppose your wife dies suddenly, unexpectedly. Will you have regrets? Are there things unsaid that should be said? Things undone that should be done?

It's time to make a change.

Husbands, love your wives. Show her today… and every day.

"Husband, love your wife." (Colossians 3:19)

---

**Discussion Questions:**

1. Do you agree or disagree that the statement, "Husband, Love your wife" is a commandment from God?"

2. Why do you agree or disagree?

3. Do you agree or disagree with the statement, "If God gives us a commandment, He gives us a way to carry it out"?

4. Why do you agree or disagree?

5. We have been told that there are 3 Greek words for "love": *eros*, *phileo* and *agape*. What is a

description of each of these loves?

6. Which do you think is the one used in Colossians 3:19?

7. Which one is not used in the Scriptures?

---

**Internal Reflection Questions:**

1. Husband, do you really love your wife?

2. Do you question whether or not you are supposed to be married to her?

3. Have you built up resentments against her? What are they?

4. Do you feel trapped and want something or someone else?

5. What regrets will you have if your wife dies suddenly?

6. Are there things unsaid that should be said? What things?

7. If you answered "yes" to any of these, what are you going to do about it?

8. What else can you do to love her more?

# FORGIVE HER

**FORGIVENESS IS TOUGH**. It's a topic we don't like to discuss and are even less likely to do. We don't like to forgive for many reasons. We are "manly." We don't like to admit our mistakes. We don't like to take the blame. We put off "facing things." We try to avoid confrontations with our wives, in part because we try to avoid pain. (We learn pretty early in our marriages that we need to keep our mouth shut in certain situations. Or at least I did). Men are very competitive. Since we are this way in sports, at work and in most areas of our lives, it is just natural for us to be competitive in our marriage. We don't like it when our wife criticizes us for the way we discipline our children, or when we make decisions with which she disagrees. Resentment builds up.

We like to keep track of wrongs our wives have done to us. We like to keep score. It makes us feel like our wives owe us something. Importantly, we use "keeping score" to justify what we are doing wrong

It is easy to think that our wives and other people don't deserve our forgiveness. Maybe they have done something terrible to us and we don't believe we can ever forgive them. There are lots of other reasons and I'm sure you have more. *So do I.*

Husbands, forgiveness is one of the MAJOR keys to having a successful, loving marriage. Lack of forgiveness often leads to divorce. I have a friend who, at some point in his marriage, had a brief affair. His wife divorced him because of it. Later on they got remarried. After a couple of years she told him she was going to get another divorce because she realized that she still could not forgive him for his affair during the first marriage. She divorced him again and as far as I know, she never forgave him before her death. Think of the trauma they went through. He was a broken man. We cried together often. Through the grace of God, my wife forgave me for my adultery. She is a shining example of God's power and love.

This whole issue of forgiveness is central in our lives, not just in our marriage. For those of you who have accepted Jesus as their personal Savior, you know what I'm going to say. For those of you who are not believers yet, please read these words and don't just skip over them. The Bible says that ALL of us have failed. The Bible calls that "sin." We all have evil thoughts and have done acts that are shameful and not up to God's standard. I know that there are people reading this who do not believe this statement. They think people are inherently good. However, if we are born good, why is it that we don't have to teach children to lie, steal or do other rotten things? They do it naturally. We are all fallen sinful creatures who will someday die and have to stand before a Holy, Just and Pure God who will judge us. Our sins will cause us to be sentenced to a life of eternal destruction. We cannot do enough good works to save ourselves because God says that even ONE sin causes us to be sentenced to eternal destruction away from His Holy presence. We need a Savior, someone who lived a perfect life, who never sinned and who died for our sins. Jesus, who was fully God and fully man (no I can't explain it nor would believe it unless it had been revealed to me by God) lived that perfect sinless life. He willingly took all our sins with Him to the cross. Crucified, not for anything He had done, but for our sinfulness. God approved His sacrifice, evidenced by Him being raised from the dead. (Yes He was. Too many people saw him). These are facts, not conjecture. Not old wives tales only believed by weak, pathetic people. Some of the greatest and most famous people who have ever lived have come to accept Jesus as who He says he is. At least six of our presidents have, as did Christopher Columbus, Isaac Newton, the Wright Brothers, Copernicus, Galileo, Isaac Newton, as well as movie stars Roy Rogers, Andy Griffith, Charlton Heston, Mark Wahlberg, Denzel Washington, Chuck Norris and many, many others.

Jesus forgave us when we were enemies of His. He didn't wait until we cleaned up our act and started being good, loving husbands. He loved us when we were unlovely. He FORGAVE us. How can we not forgive others?

I know, easier said than done. How does a son or daughter forgive their mother or father for sexually molesting them over and over, or abandoning them at an early age? How do you forgive someone for raping or murdering your wife? How did the Charleston South Carolina black church members forgive the young white man, who sat there, prayed with them, talked with them and then killed many of them? How can we forgive these people? How?

We can forgive only as an act of our will and because Jesus has forgiven us for so much more. We cannot wait until we feel like forgiving because that feeling may never come. We must set our minds to forgive. We do it as a conscious act. When every fiber of our flesh and soul cries out against the injustice they have done to us, we make a commitment to forgive them. You say,… that doesn't make sense. That's wrong. I just can't do it. But… you can. You NEED to do it. Why? For one thing, the person being hurt most by your lack of forgiveness is YOU. Then those who love you. Your lack of forgiveness leaves you angry, bitter, discouraged, defeated, stressed out and threatens your very life span. I have seen it in my own family. If you think about it, you probably have seen it in yours. Someone said "Anger, bitterness, hate and the rest, corrode its container from the inside and can only be poured out by the act of forgiveness."

You say "I still can't forgive." But you can. The Word of God commands you to forgive and when Scripture commands you to do something, you will be provided a way to do it. At some point you have to realize and be overwhelmed by God's forgiveness of you. If you have accepted Jesus as your Savior, you didn't do it after you had cleaned yourself up or after you had done a bunch of really good deeds, or after you had done better over-all than bad. You became a believer while you were an enemy of God, deep in sin and evilness. Even if you thought you were good, you were evil in God's sight. You were born into sin, lived in sin and without hope. Dead in your transgressions. But then Jesus loved you, forgave you of your sins and placed you into His family. No longer filthy in sin, but clothed in garments of salvation and wrapped in a robe of Jesus' righteousness.

You may say, "what if I don't believe in this Jesus junk?" That's OK for now, but not in the long run. You still need to forgive because YOU are the one carrying the 500 pound gorilla of unforgiveness on your back. That 500 pounds soon becomes a thousand or more and eventually becomes too much for you to carry. When you forgive others you are being set free from the bondage which surrounds you. Stop running from forgiving. Stop staying busy so you don't have to think about it. Forgive. Forgive for your own sake.

You may say "I can forgive, but I can't forget." Don't worry about that. Some people confuse the two and think forgetting is part of forgiveness, IT IS NOT. No one is asking you to forget. I don't want to forget the major sins in my life. If I did, I may do them again and I certainly don't want to go through all that pain again or worse yet put others through it. I want to remember them and use them as a reminder of just how much God has forgiven me. That said, I can tell you from experience that in some instances time has a way of causing you to forget the hurts when they are replaced by good life experiences

Two other things: Forgive yourself and forgive God. You need to do it. How do you do it? The same way you forgive others: by an act of your will. If God has forgiven you for all the mess and sin in your life, how can you not forgive yourself? I know this is not easy. I struggle with forgiving myself. I'm often reminded of some of the rotten things I have said, thought or done. Even when I know I have forgiven myself, the hurt is still there, as are sometimes the consequences. When these times come, I have to remind myself that God has forgiven me and that I have already forgiven myself. As I am reminded, I get overcome by God's grace and mercy. I am so thankful to Him.

You have to forgive God also. You may be mad at Him for taking your mother or father or other loved one away or for allowing so much suffering in the world. But God created all of us and He decides what's best. You must trust Him. You must believe He is a good God. You must believe that He has your welfare and the welfare of those you love at heart. Again, this can be difficult and I have seen people stay angry at God for the rest of their life. Question is, who is being hurt by this lack of forgiveness?

Well, what does all of this have to do with your wife? The answer is "EVERYTHING." If you keep score, hold grudges and stay angry, both of you will be miserable almost all the days of your married life. You probably will get divorced soon, or when the children leave home, or when you find someone who "understands" you better than your spouse. Then everybody suffers. You, your wife, your children, your parents, your grandparents and other extended family, and God. It's just not worth going through life with an unforgiving spirit. Make it a habit to forgive. Forgive soon after an offense, and often. It's for your own good.

You need to forgive your wife. She has forgiven you. If she hasn't, she may be waiting for you to ask for her forgiveness. Be a man. Step up. Take the lead. Show her the way. Ask her forgiveness, listing specific things you want her to forgive. These will be the things you know she has against you. For example, say "Please forgive me for not paying attention to you last night" or "Forgive me for talking ugly to you this morning. I had no right to do that."

What I am going to say next is controversial, but in most instances I think it would be best to not tell her about nor ask forgiveness for things she knows nothing about. There may be things you did prior to marrying her. There may be things you have done since marrying her. For instance, I would not tell her if you had a one night stand or a brief affair several years ago and had never been involved since then. You take it to God, ask His forgiveness and leave it at that.

I have a former friend who had an affair with a married woman. He went to the man and his wife and asked for forgiveness. The husband knew nothing about the affair until then and I believe he divorced his wife over it. There are certain things where you seek only God's forgiveness. Understood?

Keep short accounts. Not just with your wife but with everyone. FORGIVE. Do it NOW and do it often.

One other thought. Even though forgiveness is for your own good and is good for you, it will cost you something. Assuredly, the benefits far out way the costs, but when you forgive someone, you are willing to let God hand out whatever consequences He desires. You give up the right to hand out any punishment yourself. You give up the right to expect, or even request, forgiveness from others that have wronged you. Also, you have no idea how someone will respond to your forgiveness of them. They may deny that you have offended them or that they have offended you. They may get angry at you for accusing them of something. They very well may not accept your forgiveness. When you forgive, you also accept the consequences of that forgiveness.

I have a friend whose mother placed him in an orphanage at an early age. She would promise to come see him on special occasions, but did not show up. He would be so excited that she would be coming then be crushed by her failure to show up. This went on for many years. When the boy grew too old to be in the orphanage, he joined the Marines. There he accepted Jesus as his Savior. At some point God impressed upon him the need to forgive his mother, which he did. Soon after, he was back in the city where his mother lived and so he stopped by to see her. She opened the door when she heard his knock. As he stood there, he told her that he had come to see her to tell her that he forgave her for putting him in the orphanage and for not coming to see him. With that, she slammed the door in his face.

Forgiveness. It's not easy. It doesn't always get the results you want or expect. BUT, you still do it. IT IS WORTH IT!

---

**"Forgiveness" Questions:**

1.  Do you keep track of the wrongs you think your wife has done to you?

2.  Do you need to forgive her for those wrongs?

3.  Do you need to ask forgiveness for anything you have done to her?

4.  Who else do you need to forgive? What are you going to do about it?

5. Have you forgiven God?

6. Have you forgiven yourself?

# PROTECT HER

**AS I AM WRITING THIS, NEWS CAME** on about two women soldiers who have just successfully completed Army Ranger School. The first two in history. They must really be tough. They have to be, to be Rangers. I couldn't pass the training nor probably could any of you reading this. But these two women are the exception. Physically most women are just not as strong as men. Husbands, you must make sure you protect your wife as much as you possibly can. She needs to be secure in the knowledge that you will take care of her. A wife likes to be independent (on the surface) but deep down she needs to know that you love her, care for her and will do whatever you can to make her safe and secure. Believe me when I say that security is a big deal with her. When she doesn't feel protected, she feels vulnerable. She will seek protection somewhere, either within herself or with someone else. In any case, you are driving a wedge between you and her.

When I was in the midst of my affair, I sent Barbara and the boys 750 miles away to stay with her parents for a few weeks. She didn't want to go but, out of obedience to her rotten husband, she went. Not only was she away from my protection, I was the cause of her being that way. She (much later) told me how vulnerable she felt, how scared she was. Suppose something had happened to them while they were there. My guilt would have driven me crazy.

On a later occasion, she became so discouraged, mad and upset at me that she decided to leave me, to take the boys "home" to North Carolina. As she was packing her bags the Lord "told" her that if she left, she would not be under His protection, because she was leaving against His will. Quite a contrast isn't it? I had only thought about me and what I wanted to do. I hadn't really thought about God's will and my need to protect her, and yet, she obeyed God and stayed. She was protected by Him even when I wasn't protecting her. I thank God for that.

Protection comes in many forms. Hugs are a symbol of protection. I made sure I hugged my wife often. You need to do the same. I made it a point to be home with her more and not leave her alone at night if possible. I took her with me when I could and went places with her even when I wanted to stay at home. If you wife is like mine, she may be unsure about driving somewhere locally for the first time. Offer to take her or ride with her a day ahead of the time she is supposed to go. I did that often.

I am so grateful God gave me many, many opportunities to protect her during the "Great" years of our married life. I was able to show her love that way. For the last twenty plus years, four couples have been meeting every month or so to socialize and pray for each other. Needless to say, we have seen many life changes during this time. The last time Barbara was able to go, she was sitting at the dining room table with the other women in our friend's house and I had gone into the den for a little TV time with the men in the group. The women told me she kept looking for me with an anxious expression on her face. When she would see me her face would relax. I think about that time often, with both joy and great sadness. Joy because I saw visible evidence that she knew I would protect her and great sadness because I knew the dementia was becoming worse. It still hurts.

Are you acting like I used to? Hopefully not, but I know some of you are.

Husbands, protect your wives.

---

### "Protect Her" Questions:

1. Does your wife know you will protect her?

2. Are there times you have not protected her?

3. Have you asked forgiveness for those times?

4. What are some of the ways you can show her that you are protecting her?

# SERVE YOUR WIFE

**WHAT IS THIS?** What does it mean?

One of the New Testament words for "serve" means "to be an attendant, to wait upon, to minister to." Like so much of what is written here, serving is an attitude as well as an action. Develop the right attitude and your actions will follow. By serving your wife you become a giver and not a taker. More on that later.

Husbands, you need to serve your wife.

Your wife was handpicked by God to be your help-mate, your partner, your friend and confidant and the mother of your children. She is also being used by God to take the rough edges off of you, to make you into a more mature man, to make you more like what He wants you to be. She is a complex person, capable of doing many, many tasks at the same time and thinking of many different things at the same time. Most men are not like that. Men are task oriented, single minded, self-centered individuals who focus on one thing at a time. We usually don't think like a woman, nor act like a woman and we have differing needs. It's important that we realize this. We may be thinking about sex, or what's going to be happening on the next play in the football game we are watching on TV while she may be thinking about what she is going to wear tomorrow, how she is going to get the children to their different after school events, why the dishwasher isn't cleaning the dishes like it should, what the strange noise is in the car and reading a book, all at the same time. How do we cope with all that?

One of the best ways I found was to serve my wife. To develop an attitude of helping her and demonstrate that by being available when she needed something done. Too often our wives feel they are carrying the load of the family alone (and they may be). They usually are the ones who take care of the children, clean the house, cook the meals, often work outside the home, pay the bills and many other things.

Men, I came to realize that marriage is a partnership. You both have your jobs to do. Do not push them all off on her. You cannot neglect you wife. Your priority should not be working, hunting, golfing and/or watching sporting events. Your priority is first to God, then to your wife, then your children, then work. All before the hunting, fishing and golfing. You may disagree, but in the light of eternity those leisure and work activities often qualify as wood, hay and stubble. They will be burnt up.

I learned from experience (after many years of doing my own thing) as to how valuable it was to serve my wife, to help her in whatever thing she was working on with which she needed help on. As I said earlier, I helped (a little) in cleaning up the house. I took care of the boys more than I had in the past. I got her to make me a list and I did the little odd jobs she wanted to have done. We often did some of them together and that helped bring us closer. I began to take an interest in what she liked to do. She liked to cook and wanted to cook in the church kitchen, so I went with her, washed dishes and did whatever she told me to do as we served Wednesday night meals at the church. By doing this we learned to depend on each other and serve each other more. We leaned on each other more.

So often we husbands want to sit and be served, but she taught me to serve. She was a prime example of being a Jesus-like servant. In the Bible (Matthew 20:28) Jesus, speaking of Himself, said "the Son of man did not come to be served but to serve." If Jesus served others so should you. Husbands, when you serve your wife you are exhibiting Jesus to her, to your children and to others. Your children will learn to serve others which is one of the most important things they will ever learn.

Husbands, first serve your wives before you serve in public. Why is that? Public service is great. It is needed. But it's often done with the wrong motive. When you serve, you may get public attention drawn to you. That may (probably will) lead to pride and you end up serving for the wrong reason. If you are serving in public and not in your home, you are breeding dissension. She will think of you as being a hypocrite. When you serve your wife, it is generally out of the public eye. Your motive should be to show her love and support. Believe me, it pays off.

A word of caution. Make sure you serve her out of genuine love for her, not because you are trying to get something from her, or using it as a bargaining chip so she will do something for you. Don't scratch her back so she will have to scratch yours. Scratch hers without expecting anything in return. You do it because you LOVE her.

What would you regret about failing to serve her if she was to pass away today?

---

**"Serve Her" Questions:**

1. Do you serve your wife? How?

2. Are you serving out of love or because you are trying to get something from her?

3. Do you keep a list of work needed to be done around the house and do you do them?

4. List the following in priority order according to your actions: Children, work, wife, leisure activities, God.

5. Do you need to change your priorities?

6. List some things you can do on a weekly basis to serve your wife.

# BE A GIVER, NOT A TAKER

## ARE YOU A "GIVER" OR A "TAKER"?

Have you thought about yourself in these terms? Which are you? Examine yourself. This is important because your lifestyle and your actions follow the way you view life. Suppose both you and your wife are "takers." How long do you think your marriage will last unless YOU change. Suppose you are a "taker" and your wife is a "giver"? I expect that will put a great strain on the marriage and lead to a lot of resentment in your wife. The result will probably be an unhappy marriage. You need to be a giver in your marriage and also in your entire lifestyle. What is your attitude towards life? Since attitude usually determines behavior, you may need to work on your attitude. When presented with a situation or event do you think "what's in it for me?" or do you think "how does it affect others? The way you think will determine your response.

There is a huge difference between givers and takers. A taker is self- centered. A giver is other-centered. Givers do for others. Takers do for themselves. Givers encourage others. Takers don't. And the list goes on and on.

How about some examples… Having sex. When you have sex with your wife do you want to get something from her or do you want to give something to her? If you are a taker, you are interested in satisfying yourself. If you are a giver, you want to satisfy her. If you are a taker, you may treat her roughly and do to her what pleases you the most, no matter how distasteful it may be to her. If you are a giver, you do what pleases her.

Another example. Watching TV. Do you control the remote or do you ask her what she wants to watch? Now, before you get too upset about what I am saying, just remember that if there is serious disagreement let her watch what she wants to watch. Watch it with her, or watch what you want to watch on the smaller TV. Do NOT demand to watch what you want to watch.

How do you act about the meals she prepares? Do you fuss about what she cooks or do you thank her for preparing the meal? Do you help her by setting the table, or by cleaning up after the meal? Do you EVER do this? Do you offer to wash clothes or mop the floors? Or do you just sit on your butt in front of the TV while she takes care of everything?

I went to a friend's home several months ago and the house was filthy. His wife works and he doesn't. I ask you… is he a giver or a taker? Are you?

Both my mother and my wife were givers. I learned from them. Unfortunately I didn't practice a lot of that in the "Beginning" or "Doubting" years of our marriage but Barbara motivated me to follow her example and I learned to give to others and not just take. I learned to give the gift of quality time to my wife and also to my two boys. You may not realize the impact you have on your children, but if you are not a giver of time to them, you are asking for trouble. Time spent with your children is time well spent.

You do not want to get the reputation of a taker. One of my son's friends is a taker. The only time he calls my son is when he wants something. Do you do that? We all know people like that. Nobody likes a taker. A taker is self-centered and selfish while a giver is an encouragement to others. Which are you?

Be a giver. Not a taker.

---

## "Giver or Taker" Questions:

1. Are you a "giver" or are you a "taker"?

2. What evidences can you list to justify your classification?

3. Do you understand what effect each one can have on your marriage?

4. If you are a "taker," what can you do to change?

# ENCOURAGE HER

**ARE YOU AN ENCOURAGER**, or a discourager? Don't answer quickly. Think about it.

When was the last time you were an encouragement to your wife? Have you encouraged her today? Yesterday? Last week? When was the last time you were a discouragement to your wife? Which do you do more of? How about your children? Do you often tell them how special they are, or do you just criticize them for their negatives? Tragedy often results from you being a discourager. Imagine what it would be like to be treated as if you were inferior, not as talented, behind the times, not measuring up, ashamed of, looked down on and worthless. How would you feel? Do your words and/or your actions make your wife feel this way? *Never, never, never do this.* Unfortunately you may be doing this unconsciously. Please examine your attitude and your actions toward your wife and importantly, toward your children.

Early in our marriage I wasn't very good at encouraging Barbara. Fortunately, the Lord sent others to do that. When we moved to Memphis in our seventh year of marriage, we moved onto a street full of children and close neighbors who were Christians. We began going to church after my neighbors encouraged Barbara. Our children were enrolled in a private Christian school after another neighbor encouraged Barbara to enroll them there. Somehow they were accepted entrance even though I was not a believer at the time. This same neighbor encouraged Barbara to get involved in a Bible teaching church (not the church we were then going to) and in Bible Study Fellowship (BSF), where she really learned to study the Bible and to trust God. Through church members, BSF women and godly neighbors, Barbara received a great deal of encouragement, which she was not getting at home.

I also was receiving encouragement from those same sources. God put many mature, spiritual men in my life, mentoring, challenging and encouraging me. After I became a believer, one man in particular, a missionary who has a ministry of encouragement, became a very important mentor to me. Through him I learned the worth of encouraging others. As I read the Scriptures I saw many verses that talked about this very thing and saw many examples of this in the various Old Testament events. I soon realized that I, who was not an encourager, was expected to be one. So are you.

I began to encourage my wife. I made it a point to say something nice to her. I told her how much I appreciated her being such a great mom to our children and to being a spotless housekeeper. I encouraged her to get involved in activities that she wanted to be involved in but hesitant to do so. She was asked to take a children's leadership role in Bible Study Fellowship and I encouraged her in that.

She never liked to fly, much less fly long distances, but she was presented the opportunity to go on a short term mission trip to an orphanage in Brazil. I didn't want to go but I really encouraged her, as did others. (No, I wasn't trying to get her out of the house. This was after those "Dark" years.) She had such a fabulous time, she went to the orphanage six times, and to Europe twice. All without me.

I watched my wife blossom from being a "homebody" content to be at home, to becoming a world traveler. I am amazed. Much of what she did was because people came alongside her to help and encourage her. People came along side me also.

I don't know what you think of your wife. Do you think she is talented? Hard working? Or do you feel like you have left her behind? Do you think all she is interested in is the children? Are you drifting apart? Then husbands, you need to examine your attitude toward your wife. You need to find out what she is really interested in and encourage her and help her in that activity. You will be amazed at what happens when you do this.

Be an encourager to your wife, to your children, to others and watch them blossom into something great.

### "Encourage Her" Questions:

1. When was the last time you verbally encouraged your wife?

2. When was the last time you criticized your wife?

3. Do you encourage her more than you discourage her?

4. Ask the same three questions about each of your children.

5. If you are a discourager, what steps are you going to take to change?

# BE HER FRIEND

**I MENTIONED EARLIER** that we had only known each other for seven months before we were married. Those first four months Barbara lived in Raleigh, NC while I was attending school at Chapel Hill, about 30 miles away. During these months we normally saw each other only on weekends. During that summer I worked at Myrtle Beach while she was still in Raleigh, about 175 miles apart. She came to the beach some during the summer and once for a week, but we still did not spend great amounts of time together. As a result, while we thought we knew each other well, we found we did not. Like most young couples, when we got married in September, we had to adjust and adapt to each other's ways. That first year was fun. I was completing my senior year at college and she worked to pay the few bills we had. We wanted to have a child soon after I graduated, and she got pregnant in March. I graduated in May and got a job in Wilmington, NC, ten miles from one beach and about 20 from another. Life was good in those "Early" years. Only trouble was, because she was pregnant, she decided to quit drinking and dancing. That was a blow to me. Here we were, living the good life and she no longer wanted to do the things I wanted to do. Selfish me. The seeds of doubt about the marriage started at this point.

After two years in Wilmington we were transferred to the Washington DC area, and soon our second son was born. The guys I worked with often stopped for drinks after work and I usually joined them for an hour or two. The seeds of doubt continued germinating as I spent less time at home. We lived in the D.C. area for four years, after that we moved to Memphis and soon the "Doubting" years turned into the "Dark" years. I began to think that not only did I not love her, we were not even friends. We continued to grow apart, spending little time with each other. This had a terrible effect on our relationship and went on until the time that I finally committed to the marriage. After that commitment, we started doing a lot of things together and the "Great" years began. Even during the dark years we always attended the boys' soccer games and the other athletic events they were involved in. I intentionally set out to do some other fun things with the boys and with Barbara. The two of us would go to estate sales, antique stores and other places, just doing something together. I realized more and more the importance of being together and doing things together.

I was fortunate to have a wife that was hardworking. She didn't mind getting her hands dirty. We took on projects at church and at the school the boys attended.

We learned to depend on each other. When you work closely with someone and they work as hard as you or harder, you develop a trust and a friendship that grows increasingly stronger. I found there's a bonding that happens. As a result, my wife became my best friend.

Husbands, there's nothing like having your wife as your best friend. We wanted to be together, and we spent many "Great" years just enjoying each other's company. I was so blessed by her friendship. I miss that now.

There were two men at the church we attended that I always seemed to be at odds with. They opposed almost everything I proposed in our meetings. Just the sight of them tensed me up. Well, we had Saturday work days when all the leadership would get together to clean up and paint a huge building. After several Saturdays most of the work had been done and most of the men no longer showed up. Only three of us were left. You guessed it. Me and my two "enemies." We began working together and after several Saturdays of cleaning and painting bathrooms we became great friends and remained so throughout the rest of their lives. This is a prime example of what can happen when you work together.

Husbands, set your mind to make your wife your best friend. Confide in her. Do things with her that she really enjoys. If she likes to shop for antiques, shop with her. If she likes to ride around and look at the countryside, ride with her. Start working on a simple project together, something fun, something that requires cooperation and interaction. Then go on to other projects. Also, make sure you attend as many of your children's events with her as you possibly can. You will find that there are many things you really like about her. Concentrate on those rather than her negatives.

---

**"Be Her Friend" Questions:**

1. Are you friends, really good friends with your wife?

2. Do you concentrate on her negatives or on her positives?

3. Do You like to do things together?

4. Do you do more "fun" things with your wife or with your buddies?

5. What are some projects you can do together that will draw you closer to her?

# PRAY FOR HER

**HUSBAND, PRAY WITH YOUR WIFE.**

We didn't pray together much during the "Beginnings" and "Doubting" years of our marriage nor through most of the "Dark" years. But then the really hard times came starting with the boys' car wreck. As we were praying for our sons during that time we began to sense a unity. I found that something special happens when you pray regularly with someone, particularly your wife. A uniting power is unleashed, an understanding occurs. There comes a strengthening of ties. You begin to bond together. Over time your hearts just grow closer together. God wants and expects husbands and wives to live in harmony and unity with each other as like—minded people. Praying together brings that about. Someone said "Praying to God together as husband and wife brings a special unity that no other activity can accomplish. When two are joined together with God's Holy Spirit, Satan's influence and lies become helpless."

I hope it doesn't take a crisis to cause you to start praying with your spouse. It happened to us as we were tested often. For instance, the son who came out of the coma became addicted to cocaine. He is twice divorced and has tried to commit suicide three times. Fortunately Barbara and I were solidly in our marriage before any of this happened. Side Note: *That's another reason for staying together.* You never know when disease, drugs, death or other bad things are going to happen. Tragedies can strike at any time and you need to be available to help pick up the pieces and help in the restoration.

After his first divorce our son was in bad shape emotionally. It seemed as if Satan's demons were after him. He moved in with us and we cared for him (and his two children whom he got in the divorce). Every night he would start crying out, grinding his teeth and rolling around in his bed. It happened so often we set our clock and got up before two a.m., knelt beside his bed and prayed for him. It was not easy. It seemed as if a war was going on for his life and we were involved in the battle. Our weapon was prayer and we used it. Eventually, the struggling ceased. The rolling around and the teeth grinding stopped. Barbara and I came out of that experience closer together than we had ever been before. We had fought together and were victorious. Prayer, particularly prayer in times of crisis, makes you partners. It makes you warriors together.

Over the years, it just became routine to reach out to God for each other in prayer. I often failed, but many nights as we went to bed I would pray aloud for her. I know praying helped me, just as I believe it helped her. As I would pray she would hold my hand. Talk about a great feeling! Have you experienced such a time together? *Try it. You will like it.*

Husband, pray FOR your wife. Pray WITH your wife. Don't pray a prayer like "Lord, make her love me more." No, pray that she will have a good day, that she will be able to get all the things done she needs to do. Thank the Lord for putting you together. Ask Him to show you ways to support and encourage her. When you pray together do NOT make the prayer about you, make it about her. Also, she may not want to pray. That's okay. You take the lead.

---

### "Pray for her" Questions:

1. Do you know how to pray? Are you comfortable praying? *If not, ask God to show you how.* It's easy. It is just like having a conversation with a person. Tell Him whatever you like; ask him to meet whatever need you have. Praise Him.

2. Do you pray *for* your wife on a consistent basis?

3. Do you pray *with* your wife on a consistent basis?

4. Do you pray to be shown ways to serve, protect and encourage your wife?

5. Do you pray to be shown ways to make you a better husband?

# MAKE GOD CENTRAL
# IN YOUR LIVES

**HUSBANDS, I CANNOT EMPHASIZE ENOUGH** how important it is for you to commit to loving your wife by loving God first.

As Barbara and I were growing closer together in love, friendship and becoming one, we began to realize more and more how much we needed to make God and His son Jesus the focal point of our lives. We began

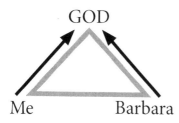

to see our lives as a triangle. A triangle with Barbara and Me at the bottom corners or base and God at the top. We found that as we drew closer to God (moving up the sides of the triangle towards God) we were automatically being drawn closer to each other. We may be growing at different speeds, but as long as we were moving up, we were being drawn closer to God and to each other.

Husbands, if you have a wife who is not interested in things of the Lord you are to pray for her. Do not nag her, do not try to make her feel guilty about it. Pray that she will desire to know God better.

This triangle works not only for marital relationships but for other relationships as well. That is one of the reasons the Bible says for us not to forsake the assembling of ourselves together. When we fellowship together and tell each other what God is doing in our lives, we are automatically being drawn closer to Him and to each other. One factor we often don't think about is who we associate with and whether or not God is central in their lives. Who do you spend time with? Who do you and your wife spend time with?

Earlier I mentioned that while we lived in Washington the guys would often go to a bar after work and have a few beers. While we were not chasing women or doing "bad" things, I can assure you that God was not central in our conversations, nor was He ever spoken of. One of my pals later divorced his wife and another committed suicide by shooting himself in the head. Now I'm not saying that us drinking together caused either but it just illustrates the lifestyle we were living. It was a life of not spending time with our families and a life without regard for godly things. Don't consistently spend time with people who lead worldly self-centered lives. They will eventually drag you down. Associate yourself individually and with married couples who desire to live wholesome, moral & godly lives. People who desire to make God central in their lives. They will be an encouragement to you and will strengthen your marriage.

---

**"Make God Central" Questions:**

1. Is God important in your life?

2. Will you ask God to give you the desire to make him more central and important in your life?

3. Will you encourage your wife to make God more important and central in her life?

4. How will you do this?

5. Name some godly couples you can get together with over a meal or sporting event, or something the children are involved in. Ask them what they do to make God central in their lives.

# COMMIT TO HER
# AND HER ALONE

I'M SURE I MEANT the "until death do us part" in our marriage ceremony and in the "Beginning" years, but that started changing during the "Doubting" years. During the "Dark" years I found I really didn't believe it. I increasingly had the thought "if things get too tough I will just divorce her." Husbands, have you had that thought? I'm sure I'm not the only one. I had a different meaning to the old saying "when the going gets tough, the tough get going." Yes, I was going. Going right out the door. Out of the marriage if it got to be too much. Obviously the self-centered me was in charge. How about you? Are you the self-centered one or the loving faithful one?

After I came to believe in the "husband love your wife" command, I committed to staying in the marriage no matter what. That meant NO DIVORCE. I could not even give myself an option to consider it. Now, I had to remind myself of this many times but in doing so I found that not having an option made me work harder to have a good marriage. If you have no options and you are in a pit with a tiger, you better try to make peace with the tiger. Funny how that commitment changes your attitude and actions. It worked for me. Hopefully it will work for you.

You do not just try to get through the tough times, you don't just resign yourself to live with the bad situation. You plan, you determine, you work at making your marriage joyous and successful. You treat your marriage as if you have no other choice, no other option. People like to say "always have a Plan B", but I say to you, you CANNOT have a Plan B.

It goes without saying, that if your life is in danger from spousal abuse or similar circumstance, you should not remain where they can harm you.

How about you? Have you really totally committed to your marriage? Or do you have a Plan B?

Husbands, commit to your wife and to her alone.

---

**"Commit" Questions:**

1. Who are or what are you most committed to?

2. Do you consider leaving your wife?
   Is it an option open to you?

3. Are you determined to make your marriage great?

4. Do you have a plan B?

# RESPECT HER

**Husbands, do you respect your wife?**
Be truthful in your answer.

My wife graduated from high school and attended a one year business college. I had an undergraduate degree and eight years later got a Masters degree. I thought I was smarter than her. (Not so in the common sense department.) At times I felt superior to her. This of course added to our problems. You may find yourself in the same situation. Often there are differences intellectually, culturally, age wise, in outlooks on life, in aggressiveness or passiveness, and many others. These differences can tear a marriage apart. They can cause you to lose respect for your mate and that can create serious consequences.

I hope you don't find yourself in a similar situation. If you do, you must change. Don't waste time mentally recounting the ways you are "better" than her. That is just a path that leads to destruction. It becomes much easier when you spend the majority of your time focusing on your wife's good qualities and very little on her negatives. For instance, when you are in a group just talking and she says something you think is really stupid, do NOT criticize her and do not just be silent if at all possible. Turn what she said into something positive. That way she has visible evidence of you supporting and respecting her.

After I committed to our marriage, I realized this lack of respect had been a big part of my problem with Barbara. I knew I had to change my attitude. I began to dwell on the positives in her. I've already mentioned some of them. She was hard working, faithful, trustworthy, full of common sense, friendly, compassionate and loved our children. I could rely on her to do what she said she was going to do. She was very dependable.

I began to ask her opinion on problems I was having at work. I found she had great insight (most women do). She was a big help to me.

As I continued to focus more attention on her positives and less and less on her negatives, my respect for her grew enormously. I saw beauty in her that I had not seen before. I discovered that she had fantastic qualities. I became very proud of her and became more and more thankful that we were together.

Look at your wife with a different attitude. Look for her good qualities and compliment her on them. While you are at it, tell her how much you appreciate her. Husbands, do it often.

## "Respect Her" Questions:

1. Do you truly respect your wife?

2. What annoys and frustrates you about her?

3. Will you be determined to think more about her positives than her negatives?

4. Will you commit to continually compliment her on her positives and not criticize her?

# COMMUNICATE WITH HER

**I STARTED TO WRITE** "Talk with her" but realized that doesn't describe what needs to happen. You need to talk WITH and LISTEN TO your wife. That's either implied or stated in almost everything I have written. An old joke is told about a husband complaining that "My wife says I never listen to her… at least that's what I think she said."

It is so simple but just doesn't happen in so many marriages. That was another one of our problems. Barbara and I did not communicate well with each other. We had different interests and different thought processes. My wife sometimes had a critical spirit which would be accentuated because she often spoke without thinking. What came out of her mouth could be offensive. I found it was best for me to keep my mouth shut. Arguing wouldn't help, it would only increase the tension. Plus, she was always telling me what I was thinking, or at least what she thought I was thinking. That would make me angry. She would accuse me of all sorts of things that had never entered my mind.

I know some of you find yourself in the same situation. In the past week I have had two men tell me they just don't talk to their wives. It's easier on them because a lot of what is said gets misunderstood. When they speak, the emotions begin to flow and the arguments begin; so in their mind it's just best and easier to keep quiet.

Also this past week I have seen quite a communication contrast. I have a Galaxy cell phone. My college age grandson has an iPhone. In my technologically challenged state I had never seen anyone use Facetime. I was amazed. My grandson spent an hour doing Facetime with his best friend (male) at the Naval Academy. He then spent forty five minutes with a friend (female) over six hours away at Auburn University. They talked continuously. They were excited. They were interested in what each other was doing. Now, I can hear you thinking "that's because they are far away and don't talk to each other often." Not so. Not so. Auburn gets a call every night. Every night.

What would happen if we did that with our spouses? What would happen if we did Facetime with them? How much different would our marriages be?

Husbands, learn to talk with your wife. I had to do so—so do you.

It may be difficult to begin. Find something you both enjoy and agree on. Talk about that. If you think you have nothing in common, then talk about something in which she has an interest. Let her do most of the talking. And when she is talking, PAY ATTEN-TION and respond with simple, positive comments that show her you have been listening.

Take an interest in her world. Also, you need to be involved in her world. It is up to you to take the lead in this and all the other areas we have talked about.

Husbands, you are supposed to be the head of the family. Take the initiative, lead and don't sit back. Start conversations, even when you do not feel like talking.

---

## "Communicate" Questions:

1. How is communication between you and your wife? Good? Bad? Non-existent?

2. Do you often get into arguments because one of you thought you had told the other one something?

3. Do you or your wife often misunderstand what the other has said?

4. Do you pay attention when she is talking to you?

5. Do you take an interest in her life, as to what she is thinking, feeling or doing?

6. How can you make communication between you two better?

# MAKE LOVE TO HER

**EVEN THOUGH** I have placed this last, I realize sex can be one of the biggest stumbling blocks in a marriage as well as one of its greatest joys. It is so important, yet I have felt led to share only a few brief statements about what I have learned. Dwell on these words, add to them.

I learned to make love to my wife, not just have sex with her. There is a difference.

I learned that in order for me to make love to my wife and not just have sex with her I needed to be patient, to be kind, to be gentle and to have self-control.

I learned that sharing our bodies was God's gift to us, given to help unify us both physically and emotionally.

I learned that I should try to meet her needs and in doing that, my needs would be met.

I learned that my focus needed to be on her, not on me.

I learned what she liked and didn't like and did what she liked.

I learned to be sober, washed and clean.

I learned to take my time.

I learned that giving her pleasure gave me pleasure.

What about you? If you are just having sex, stop it.

Start making love.

# LAST WORDS

**I KNOW THERE ARE OTHER POINTS** to make and other ways I have been affected by my life with Barbara but this is enough for now. Husbands, I also know that you are capable of finding other ways to grow closer and more in love with your wife.

My aim in writing these words has been to encourage you, to make you think about the way you treat and respond to your mate. I encourage you to act, to work hard at your marriage, to perhaps look at your marriage in a different light. Your wife is a treasure, a gift from God. If you are not sure about that and are struggling right now, please take these words to heart.

I had to learn the hard way and I cannot begin to express the depths of the pain I caused Barbara, my immediate and extended family, my girlfriend, her family, myself, and others. To say I regret the "Dark" years and covet the "Great" years does not come close to convey the range, depth and height of emotions I experience now that Barbara is gone.

Fortunately, God in His mercy and grace kept us together and I am so thankful and blessed for the many wonderful and "Great" years we had together, I am sure that I will see Barbara again in God's kingdom. Not only that, but I will be with her for eternity. This gives overwhelming joy to my heart and helps cover the sweet sorrow of grief that misses her now. I'm reminded that eternity is a long period of time.

Life on this earth is short. My prayer is that when you get to my age you will be able to look back on your lives together as being the best years of your lives.

It's time to start.

It's time to change.

Husbands, do it now.

*Before she is gone.*

## FaceBook entry June 6, 2015

Barbara's grave marker was placed on her grave the other day. I went by Wednesday to look at it and make sure everything was spelled right (it was). Thanks to my buddy Scott who got it taken care of. It's a great looking marker. Classy. Just like Barbara was. To the point. Just like Barbara was. A bible and a cross. Two things Barbara really thought a lot of and talked about a lot. She loved Jesus. She loved what He had done for her in saving her. Living a perfect sinless life, taking her sins with Him to the cross and being resurrected gave her faith that she would be with Him. And I know she is. I rejoice and am so thankful for the Lord putting her into my life. She was the greatest example of Jesus' unconditional love and forgiveness I know. I know because she loved me and forgave me and I didn't deserve it. It was her love for me that caused her to send Pastor

Steven's to our house, where the Lord used him to lead me to Jesus. It was her obedience to her Lord that she did not leave me or divorce me. Her forgiveness of me made me love her all the more… and the Lord also. I miss her, but rejoice so much because she has been set free from the terrible scourge of dementia.

While I was looking at the marker, I was struck by the sight of my name being there. "A. Russell, October 27,1940—." I don't believe most of you have experienced seeing your own name on a grave marker—only those who have been through what I have—and I tell you, *it is a sobering experience*. Even though I look forward to being with her in heaven, the reality of my impending death hit me again. I so don't want to end my race of life badly. I know what I am capable of and I just want to cling to Jesus and lean on Him to protect me from the evil one. That said, I know I have been left here for a reason and that reason is not to try to just end life without stumbling, God has left me here to proclaim his goodness, His glory, His forgiveness of sins. May I be about His business in the days I have left.

Come to think about it,… you are still here on this earth. That means God has a purpose for your life. What are you doing? What will you do? Something to think about because one day you will be where I am.

Made in the USA
San Bernardino, CA
21 June 2016